I love
I hope you
true all
that. -Brury

the little book of
STANDUP

by John Vorhaus

Copyright © 2022 John Vorhaus

No part of this book may be reproduced or transmitted in any form or by any electronic or mechanical means, including photocopying, recording, teleporting, telepathy and alien abduction, or by any information storage and retrieval system including carving in stone without the express written permission of the author, except where permitted by law.

Cover design by the author

All rights reserved

Published in the universe by Bafflegab Books

www.bafflegabbooks.com

Bafflegab Books

SOME BOOKS BY JOHN VORHAUS

Lucy in the Sky

Creativity Rules!

The California Roll

The Comic Toolbox

How to Write Good

Comedy Writing 4 Life

The Albuquerque Turkey

A Million Random Words

the little book of SITCOM

A White Belt in Art

Poole's Paradise

The Texas Twist

how to live life

there are more

to you who are on the road

the little book of
STANDUP

contents

INTRODUCTION~ i
1~ A WHITE BELT IN STANDUP 1
2~ THE START OF GOOD PRACTICE 7
3~ OUCH MY FEELINGS 13
4~ COMIC FILTERS 24
5~ AWARENESS 30
6~ AUDIENCE 37
7~ THE HOPE MACHINE 43
8~ STATUS 54
9~ STUCK... 63
10~ LET'S BUILD A BIT 72
11~ PRACTICAL JOKES 80
12~ FIRST FIVE 81
13~ *POCHEMU NYET?* 87
14~ SET YOURSELF A CHALLENGE 94
15~ HAPPY WHERE YOU ARE 101

INTRODUCTION~ JV IS A BROBDINGNAGIAN FORCE

by Ashley Whimsy Gutermuth

Okay, first off, my middle name is not Whimsy, but we'll get back to that. I am a standup comic but also I am clinically obsessed with comedy. I grew up watching and impersonating comedians as much as I possibly could, which was constantly. Maybe you have that streak in you, too. It seems to come with the territory.

My relationship with John Vorhaus (henceforth known as JV by his own incessant insistence) began like all healthy relationships, over the internet. I still don't know if he actually exists beyond a Zoom screen. We started talking after I bought his book *A White Belt in Art* from his website, which you also should totally do, and this is me, Ashley, saying that, not JV editing me after the fact (editor's note: actually, it is). Anyway, JV, being an enthusiastic reacher-outer, sent me an email thanking me for giving him money so that he could buy more Ultimate Frisbee discs. I haven't bought anything from him since because I refuse to enable any sport where the equipment doubles as a dinner plate. Though I shouldn't be the one to talk. After all, I run miles every day picking up roadside trash, my own little adopt-a-highway program.

Which JV didn't find strange, so we hit it off right away.

When the talk turned to comedy, a subject of avid common interest, we arranged to meet once a week across the aether (that's a JV spelling of a JV word — more on that in a sec) to work on our work. Why he wanted to meet with me I don't know. Lots of people treat me like something that would be interesting to keep in a jar to look at later, so I just assumed that was the case. But for me, in my ongoing quest to get all the information I can from anyone with a comic mind, I was more than willing to meet with this effervescent sexagenarian. Yes, effervescent, and yes, sexagenarian; what can I tell you? There's something about JV that makes you want to use big words. Maybe it's competition, a spirit of one-upmanship. Where I'd be all *grand* or *grandiose*, he'd be *whopping*, which I would simply have to top with *towering*, and then he'd bring *humongous*, so then I'd be *gargantuan* and he *Brobdingnagian* and it just went on and on.

Some sessions we didn't get a lot of work done.

JV is the only person I've ever met who can't help but write in his own voice. It pours out of him like oil from the crankcase of my '98 Buick. Some people have to find their voice but JV has to tell his to shut up. By nature he is a bold person. He'll just move into something, make something of it, and then move on to the next thing. Play professional poker? You bet. Write sitcoms? Insert studio audience. Teach standup? Laughable. "But who better to teach than an avid learner?" JV would insist. He may be right. You'll know soon enough.

I already knew his work as the lead mechanic of his book *The Comic Toolbox: How to be Funny Even if You're Not* and also from his exceedingly cheeky *A Million Random Words*, which is, in fact, nothing but a million random words, or a million and four if you count the title, but then it would be, like, actually *A Million and Six Random Words*, and this is just the sort of rabbit hole JV draws you down, and I mean that in a good way.

So we got along well, me and JV, henceforth known as John because I'm capricious. He's a fair dose of whimsy, and whimsy as it happens is my middle name. Ashley Whimsy Gutermuth.

Gosh, if only that were true. "Thanks," I would say. "Thanks, Mom and Dad for that top-shelf middle name."

I was interested to see what he had to say about the structure of comedy but soon found myself down the rabbit hole (did I mention rabbit holes?) of his deceptively simple takes on things ("don't fear bad outcomes," is an example that comes to mind) and stories of his life. Did you know that this world expert on comedy is also a world class educational consultant? He also made TV shows in Nicaragua and ran the writing staff of the Russian version of *Married... with Children*. I mean, c'mon.

Basically, John has hacked life. He inherently knows that the quickest way to get better at something is to do it, fail, learn, do it again. The rules don't much matter to him. John won't tell you that prop comedy sucks or not to bring a guitar on stage. He'll say try it and see. I feel the same way. Let's not throw a bunch of rules around things. Let's just "throw it out the window and see if it lands," as JV would say and has said, and yes I'm back to calling him JV because some people, you know, they're just not Johns.

When I met JV, he was just starting to write the book that you are now holding in your hands or reading on your phone. Within a few months, he'd basically written the whole thing. That is pretty frustrating. What kind of irritating monster actually gets things done? He didn't waste time wondering or doubting. He just wrote. I write every day but then I spend God's own time rewriting, tuning, trying to get each joke just right. Now here's JV, and he's written enough books to fill an Ikea bookcase (the big one, the Oxberg) because he just goes. When he's on fire, he writes. When he's puzzled or lost, he just writes. When he's disgruntled (or even fully gruntled), he keeps writing. I love that approach, and have adopted it like a mile of highway. Now when I can't find a joke, I just splash words in all directions – whatever is true for me – knowing that eventually I'll write something that does what I need it to do. JV taught me how to forget impediments and just keep going. For me, that's the main takeaway. Just keep going.

JV just keeps going. He writes, he paints, he still plays ultimate, which blows my mind. Doesn't he know he's a flipping sexagenarian? Maybe not. He says that his motto for his golden years is *finish hard*. I guess that's the key to success.

Finish hard.

Go hard.

Keep creating. There's at least a million and six random jokes in the world, all just waiting to be picked up and played with. The more you play, the more the comedy gods will smile on you, for they will see that you are using what they give you. Comedy gods are no fools. They don't waste their goodies on someone who waits until it's perfect to bring it into the world. Don't wait! Be like JV! Go hard! Keep giving them you until you is what they want! That's the path to standup success or my middle name ain't Whimsy.

Wait, what?

Ashley Gutermuth
@AshGutermuth
AshleyGutermuth.com

1~ A WHITE BELT IN STANDUP

A few years back, I took up art for the first time. Right from the start I knew I was gonna kinda suck. I mean, how could I not? I was doing something I'd never done before. To protect myself from self-consciousness, I decided to go for "a white belt in art," because the white belt is the one they give you for just showing up. I figured that was something I could easily do: just show up.

What I had done, of course, was to set my expectations nice and low, and easy to exceed. This got me where I wanted to go, over the hump of my own insecurity and into an active practice of art.

That was and is a good approach and I bet it can work for standup comedy, too. I bet if you set your expectations nice and low, and then exceed them, you'll find yourself over whatever insecurities you may have, and deeper into the great game of making people laugh.

You say you don't have insecurities?

Don't make me laugh.

You have them. I have them. We all have them. But we can all overcome them by setting a low bar – even one as low as "just show up." Why? Because lower expectations equal less pressure, and when pressure is reduced, it's easier to perform better in every sense: writing, editing, booking, promotion and of course actually doing your thing onstage.

So that answers one question right away.

How can I get better at my practice of standup?

Just lower expectations.

But this raises another question: *Where am I in my practice right now?* You've got to be somewhere, right? I mean, otherwise why are you reading this book?

Maybe you're *on the verge* of your practice: You haven't done standup yet, but you want to and you're finding your way in.

Maybe you've acquired some seasoning already. Maybe you've performed enough times that the mere thought of taking the stage doesn't make you want to barf into your backpack.

Maybe you've been at it a long time and you're a pro – actually getting paid for your sets. If that's you, that's great. You're much farther along in your practice than you were when you first started out.

Wherever you are in your practice, I'm going to try my best to help you advance.

If you're just starting out, I want to help you get your feet wet.

If you're growing in your craft, I want to help you grow faster.

If you're a veteran, I want to help you make the most of what's already working for you.

And if you're for sure *not a standup comic* – someone who thinks, "You know, standup isn't really for me but I wouldn't mind reading a book on the subject" – well maybe I can trick you into having a practice, too. Because I know you want to. I just know you do.

Anyway, no matter where you are in your practice, here are the things I'm going to try to provide:

> ➢ Tools
> ➢ Inspiration
> ➢ Awareness

The tools will help you write more jokes and better jokes, and give you useful insight into what parts of your comedy work for you and why. This may also help reduce insecurity just by equipping you with new approaches that yield good results.

The inspiration will come – well, I hope it will come – from the knowledge that your standup comedy contains a tremendous amount of personal power: power to make people laugh; power to make them think; power to change the world.

And awareness? I've always thought of awareness as "the one thing that fixes everything." Can it be otherwise? The better you know and understand yourself and everyone around you, the better you're going to do at anything, including standup.

Not that all of this doesn't require some leaps of faith on your part.

If I present you with new tools, you're going to have to convince yourself that tool-driven creativity is better than magic creativity, or at least a worthy partner to it.

If I seek to inspire you to embrace the power in your work, you're going to have to persuade yourself that such power exists, that you can have it, and that you are entitled to use it.

And if I say to you that awareness is the one thing that fixes everything – so touchy-feely, so California – you might have to fight the urge to laugh me right out of my own book.

Fortunately, there's a way to make these leaps of faith that doesn't require any real work on anyone's part. Just tell yourself that the thing that you *want* to be true *is* true. This is called a **useful fiction** and it works like this: A guy comes along (this guy here) and says to you, "Hey, these tools and strategies and ideas of mine are going to help you be a better standup comic." You don't *believe* believe, but you play along anyhow, because at least a part of you wants to give these tricks a try. And with that you've shifted your thinking from *this can't possibly work* to *hey, maybe it will.*

That's a big win right there. That gets you out of a negative mindset and into a positive one. And how did you get there? You told yourself a lie... *admitted* it was a lie... but told it anyhow, for the sake of the benefit you hope it will bring.

Probably this is a strategy you already use. Maybe you use it to find the courage to go up on a new and scary stage. Or maybe to write something bigger and more challenging than you've written before. Or steel yourself to approach a booker who you just *know* is going to tell you no. Any time you invest hope in anything, you're invoking a useful fiction. You don't *know* it's going to work out, but you *hope* it will work out, and telling yourself that it *will* work out puts you halfway into the place where it *can* work out.

That's a lot to take on, I know. Pretty heady stuff, and I don't expect it to make sense all at once. So let's just put it this way: What have you got to lose?

Only the cost of this book, and that's not much. Plus your time, of course. You don't want to be seen wasting your time, and I get that. But I put it to you that if you work with the ideas in this book and get *no fricking improvement whatsoever*, you'll still be ahead of the game because you will have spent a certain amount of time trying to get better – and spending time trying to get better is exactly, one hundred percent, the way to get better all the time.

RECAP

> ➢ Lowering expectations improves performance
> ➢ Awareness is the one thing that fixes everything
> ➢ A useful fiction is a fiction, but it's useful just the same

2~ THE START OF GOOD PRACTICE

I'm not a famous guy. I have climbed the pinnacle of celebrity all the way to game show appearances and a certain modest prominence at my local Starbucks, where I'm know as *That Author Guy* or, alternatively, *Mr. Tall Two Pumps Extra Foam Caramel Latte*. But let's face it, for the roughly eight billion people living on the planet today, almost exactly all eight billion of them have never heard my name.

For people who *have* heard of me, it's usually because of my book *The Comic Toolbox: How to be Funny Even if You're Not*. I wrote that book way back in the last century and I'm happy to say that all these years later it's still out there helping comedy writers and other writers do their thing. Probably it will still be chugging along long after I'm dead, buried and gone, which is a humbling thought, but also an inspiring one.

It's nice to know that I've done something of lasting impact in my life.

It's not the only thing I've done, though, not by a long shot. Among my many crazy careers and careerlets I can count advertising copywriter, folk singer, mime, ventriloquist, temp typist, sitcom writer and head-writer, face painter, lifestyle journalist, talk show host, screenwriter, novelist, audience warm-up guy, color commentary guy, creative consultant, educational consultant, marketing consultant, con artist, digital artist, art artist, nude model, network executive in charge of production and, get this, an authority on poker to the tune of ten books.

If life is an amusement park ride – as I fancy it is – I have certainly not wasted my go.

But for all of the fulfilling, diverting or deranged things I've done in my time, there's one thing that I haven't done nearly as much as I'd like, and that's standup comedy. It's an itch that I'd always wanted to give a good scratching to. Then the COVID-19 pandemic and Zoom mics came along and I realized I could scratch it at last, as much as I liked, right in the privacy of my own home, naked from the waist down.

So I started doing standup. Sitdown standup.

I had a lot to learn.

Fortunately, I have a strategy for that. Whenever there's something I want to learn, I find some way to teach it.

I've done this all my life. With songwriting and screenwriting. Networking and public speaking. Comedy, art and – scarily, perilously – archery and sailing. Sometimes it turns into books; I think I only ever wrote all those poker books because I was trying to deepen my own understanding of the game.

But as I said at the time (and it's absolutely true), "As a poker player, I'm a pretty good writer." I never came close to mastering poker, but I had a knack for helping others improve their game, and that's the knack I'm going to try and use here. Because if I ever, for an instant, tried to leverage my authority as a "master of standup," well then you *would* laugh me out of my own book, and rightly so. No, what I am is a keen student – a keen student who, as it happens, learns by teaching.

And the first thing I learned about standup was about my **voice**.

In artistic terms, voice is the thing that an artist wants to say and the way they have of saying it. Like when Picasso painted *Guernica*, he was using his anti-war voice.

In standup, when people who think you're funny tell you you're funny, that's what they're talking about: your voice; your bent perspective; your "you" way of looking at the world.

Why does this matter? For one thing, because there's so many other standups out there. They all can do jokes that anyone can do.

But they can't do jokes that only you can do!

If you know your voice, you know your truth, but also you know your brand. You can start to set yourself apart. That's kind of a big deal.

I was a baby at standup. I didn't know my voice. So I lined up my jokes and I asked of each one, "Could any standup comic tell this joke, or really just me?"

Like, "You don't find a time machine every day, but if you had one you certainly could." That's me for sure, all conceptual an' shit.

On the other hand, my idea for a post-pandemic musical, "Ouchie, Dr. Fauci," that sounds like a joke anyone could tell.

Do this a bunch of times with a bunch of your jokes and you start to get clarity on where your real standup strengths and interests lie.

Are you the sort of standup who can get ten jokes out of today's news? You have a *voice* in current events.

Do you make up words like I do? Condolulations, you have *voice* in verbal shenanigans.

Do you like to shock people? Holy queefing shit, you have *voice* in busting taboos.

Where do you think your voice lies? Which of your jokes make you feel funny *and* authentic? Line them up and inspect them for voice. Don't ask which are good, or even which you like best. Those are value judgments and we don't need those right now. Right now we just want to know which jokes are closer to our voice and which are further away.

When we take this approach – evaluate, don't judge – we step outside the whole ego thing of *oh, this joke works and I rule but that joke sucks and I drool.*

And with this I reveal my not-so-hidden agenda: to help you step outside the whole ego thing, as part of your growth toward a better practice of standup. I'm not saying it's easy, but now at least we have a method for being objective. We can look at jokes we've written or are writing, and not say that these are good or those are bad but just, "What do we have here?"

There's so much benefit in just asking, "What do we have here?" It gets you out of your ego and into your growth.

So there's two things going on here. One is the effort to deepen your understanding of what is and is not your voice. The other is building the habit of looking at your own work impartially, almost scientifically. If you do these two things, you will soon come both to know and to accept yourself and your material that much better.

And that's the start of good practice.

RECAP

- Your voice is an asset that you can identify and grow
- You can easily determine which jokes fit your voice
- Objectivity makes creativity work

3~ OUCH MY FEELINGS

When someone doesn't laugh at your joke, how do you feel? Does their rejection hurt your feelings? A lot of standups get into that head. It makes it hard for them to perform well because they're so hooked on scoring approval points and so miserable when they don't. They experience the failure of a joke as the end of the world. They suffer – but they don't seek clarity. They waste time wishing the audience would "get them" and resenting the clueless bastards when they don't.

I'm not into that. When a joke doesn't work, I try to sail right past "How do I feel?" and straight into "How do I fix this?" When my ego impedes me – as anyone's will – I try to overwhelm it with the sheer joy of fixing broken jokes. Copping this attitude of "see a problem, solve a problem" helps me look at my jokes honestly, find what needs to be fixed, and set about fixing it without stubbornness, resentment or fear.

Okay, so here we have a strategy – treat unfunny jokes as problems to be solved, not threats to our feelings – now all we need are some tactics. Here are some that I favor.

Shuffle the keyword. A joke, as you know, is a puzzle that the audience solves. When they solve the puzzle suddenly and explosively, the explosion you hear is a laugh. The **keyword** is the word or phrase that triggers all this, the final piece of information that solves the puzzle of the joke.

Take a moment to look at your jokes (ones that work and ones that don't) (lots of both) and see where the keywords are. Often a joke doesn't work simply because the keyword is out of place. So that's a simple fix. Just move it around till you find where it fits.

Usually it fits at the end, because setup before punchline, right? Here are some one-liners with the keywords last.

*When you think about it, all marriages are same-sex marriages. Year after year, **same sex**.*

*When I see a pill bottle with the words, "Alcohol may intensify effect," I think, yay, **instructions!***

*Scratch the surface of a Californian and what do you get? **More surface.***

The setup poses a question. The punchline – the keyword – answers the question in a surprising way. If the audience is appropriately taken by surprise, they crisply solve the puzzle of the joke and they laugh.

Part of what makes this happen is **tension** – the listener's sense of anticipation in wondering where the joke is headed.

An audience hears, "Scratch the surface of a Californian and what do you get?" and suddenly they're thinking, "Well, what *do* you get?" Then here comes the answer – *more surface* – and now, in a flash, they have enough information to solve the puzzle of the joke.

If, that is, they happen to know that Californians are thought to be superficial.

But what if they don't know this? In that case, just…

Add information. If the audience doesn't understand your joke, they won't laugh. That's a given. But you can aid their understanding by giving them clues in the setup. You don't have to be heavy-handed about it, just slide the information in there for the people who need it. Here's that Californians joke again, with context added.

I'm not saying Californians are shallow, but scratch the surface of one and what do you get? More surface.

Adding information adds clarity; it also adds tension. Not the tension of "where is this headed?" but emotional tension between the topic of the joke and the teller's feelings about it. You can add tension to your joke just by highlighting the relationship you have with your subject, as here...

I grew up in California, lived there all my life, but I don't always feel at home there. People are so superficial. It's like, scratch the surface of a Californian and what do you get? More surface.

The tension is found in the phrase *I don't always feel at home there.* That's when the joke becomes less about *it* and more about *you.* It's also where the joke acquires a point of view, otherwise known as **attitude**.

Attitude is just your opinion, but stated in a way that makes it clear how you're at war with your subject. Just as you always have the option of adding more clues to the puzzle, you always have the option of loading more attitude in.

Try expanding some of your jokes in this way. Add the information and attitude that will give the audience a better sense of what you're driving at. Seek to have setups that provide full context and also build real tension.

When you start monkeying around with jokes in this way – creating different versions, adding or subtracting information – you start to see that jokes are not fixed and rigid things. They're dynamic and fluid; they change. Be willing to change – excited to change – and you'll stay more alive in your craft, more flexible, more growth-oriented and more self-aware. That's a lot... quite a lot. And you get it all just by tinkering with your jokes and tuning them as you like.

Subtract information. When you give the audience too much information, you leave them with no challenging puzzle to solve; the puzzle solves itself and goes *pfft*. This can happen for a lot of reasons. Maybe their expectation isn't fooled. Maybe the punchline is too obvious or telegraphed. Maybe the misdirection doesn't legitimately misdirect. Maybe the setup is way overdone.

Usually the way to fix this is just to cut words and keep cutting them until you find a sharper way to tell the joke. To some people, this can feel a little like killing their cherished children – *"I wrote these words! They're mine and they're precious!"* – but we're all about *see it, solve it* now, right? So let's watch what happens when we clear out the clutter.

Here's a first version of a joke.

I'm getting older now and I'm afraid that I might get Alzheimer's disease. If that happens, I could end up being a big burden to my family and I don't want that. So I came up with a plan. First I put together a lethal dose of sleeping pills and placed them in my night table drawer. Then I wrote a note and put it in there, too, and the note read, "Dear Mr. Vorhaus, enclosed please find these pills. In the event you discover that you no longer remember what they are for, please consume them all."

That's fairly overstated. Let's make some cuts.

The threat of Alzheimer's is real in my life and I don't ever want to be a burden to my family. With that in mind, I've put together a lethal dose of sleeping pills and put them in my nightstand, along with a note that reads, "Dear JV, one fine morning you will wake up and find that you can't remember what these pills are for. That would be a good time to take them."

Actually, this version is a little misleading because it only suggests, but doesn't order, the suicide. Softening the instruction both confuses the situation and sucks a lot of tension out of the setup. So let's take another pass.

I don't want me and my crappy memory to ever be a burden to anyone, so what I've done, I've put together a lethal dose of sleeping pills and stuck 'em in my nightstand, along with a note that reads, "When you forget what these are for, take them."

That's a tighter telling of the joke, arrived at through aggressive editing. Of course I can always go too far – cut out information that the audience actually needs, or even just enjoys, but as a useful rule of thumb, always be thinking shorter, shorter, shorter. **When in doubt, cut things out**.

Are you concerned that if you cut too much you'll come up short and won't have enough material to fill up your set? You don't have to worry about that. You're in your practice, now; you can have all the jokes you need. Still, a lot of comics fall by this wayside. They think, "I've only got these precious few jokes so I'd really better stretch them out." But this just means that they're padding their act with *chuffa* – with stuff that's not funny, doesn't build tension and just takes up space.

Think of a joke as a coded message. You deliver the message when you tell the joke. The audience decodes your words into meaning and, if all goes according to plan, then they laugh. The more strategically you encode your joke, the more powerfully it pops and the harder it lands. So be strategic. Prize effectiveness over self-indulgence. Pride yourself on the surgical precision of your work. Boil your jokes down to pure information. *What's the setup? What's the punchline? What's this other part over here?* If it's not setup and it's not punchline, then it's just chuffa – filler – and you can cut it 'cause you really don't need it.

Here's my cure for Alzheimer's: a lethal dose of sleeping pills and a note that reads, "When you forget what these are for, take them."

The most extreme form of cutting, of course, is cutting the whole joke. Hey, it happens. In the name of improving your act, you and some jokes are just going to have to part ways. But look, if a joke is dull and you're reluctant to admit it, don't be. Replacing a dull old joke with a sharp new one is never a bad deal, and don't forget that all the jokes you write, even ones you later change or cut loose, contribute to your body of work and therefore contribute to your growth.

Change information. I love to crack myself up. Sometimes I feel like if the joke is funny to me, I don't care whether the audience gets it or not. That can be a healthy attitude to have – what fun is it to tell jokes that even I don't like? – but not if it goes too far. For me it goes too far when I get hooked on a version of a joke just because I like how it sounds or how it works for me. I forget that I'm not my audience, and that I can't place my self-pleasuring (I don't mean that like it sounds) ahead of my mission of spreading mirth and meaning wherever I can. I stray from my path when my work becomes less about serving the needs of my audience and more about showcasing the wonderfulness that is me.

I return to my path by scouring my material for *wrong information*: jokes or parts of jokes that are obscure, bland, confusing, self-serving or irrelevant.

Here are some types of wrong information I've indulged in, and maybe you have, too.

"But it really happened that way!" Many of our best jokes flow from our lived experience. Some standups feel this can only work if they stick to the facts, or make sure to share all the facts. Trouble is, details that "prove it really happened" just take up space. We need to be free to explore what's genuinely funny and emotionally essential about our experiences, even if that means loosening our grip on the particulars. It helps to remember that no one cares if you're truthful, just so long as you're real. What's the difference between truthful and real? Truthful is *what happened.* Real is *why it mattered.* Be creative with the former but loyal to the latter, and you'll be on the right track.

"Then you must be stupid!" This one night I told my wife a joke and she said, "I don't think that's funny." I blurted out my reply, "Then you must be stupid," and, predictably, spent the night on the couch. Obviously my mistake was protecting my ego by blaming my audience for not liking my joke, and I've worked hard to learn not to do that. What I try to focus on is this: Jokes belong in my act because they *work*, not because I *want* them to work or refuse to admit that they don't.

"But it worked before!" Sometimes, when material is fresh and new, it seems to work just *because* it's fresh

and new. Maybe the topic is trending hot or maybe your performance is energized by your infatuation with the new bit. However, both heat and newness wear off over time, and then it gets hard to know whether the material still works or we just think it works because we remember that it worked before. Of course the audience will tell us by their reaction, but only if we listen – which, often, we do not. We dig in our heels with the petulant mindset of, "This other audience loved that joke, how come you clowns do not?" Don't let force of habit drive your act. Make all of your material keep earning its keep.

"Why don't they get me?" Sometimes we expect the audience to think like we think, know what we know, have our same cultural literacy or frames of reference. That can't ever work for me because my references include everything from the Siege of Münster in 1534 to the television debut of *The Munsters* in 1964. I can't expect everyone to know what I know. But what I can do, if they don't get a joke, is just fix it if I can or chuck it if I can't. No more lying awake nights wondering why my Bernhard Knipperdolling jokes don't land. (If you knew about the Siege of Münster, you'd *howl!*) Maybe that's for the best, for if other people had to live inside *my* mind, I'm pretty sure their heads would explode.

Fundamentally, all jokes are built from *information.* Our awareness of this helps us step outside of attachment to old or imperfect versions of jokes and pure information management, thing more or less than to make as it can.

- eat jokes as information
- Tune your jokes like tuning a radio
- Be strategic; serve the work

4~ COMIC FILTERS

People often speak of the magic of creativity – the sense that ideas come to us from outside or beyond ourselves. I love magic as much as the next guy (unless the next guy is Siegfried or Roy) but I never want to have to rely on magic for my jokes. Magic is just too fickle that.

You know how this works: You're walking down the street when from out of nowhere – *bam!* – you're struck by something funny and now you're off and running with a new bit.

But what about the many, many other times when you're walking down the street and you don't get struck like that? What do you do then? Then you use tools. Magic comes and goes, but tools are always there.

Here's a tool that's always been there for me: the **comic filter.**

A comic filter is a special way of processing reality. You'll always find it where you find your *voice* – in the spaces where friends find you funny – but that's not the only place to look. Basically any quirk or characteristic of your personality or outlook can be turned into a strong comic filter.

Like, we already know that some people find me funny because I use language in unusual and sadlarious ways. I have that quirk of perspective, that comic filter. But it's not the only one I have. Other filters of mine include – off the top of my head – *liberal, energetic, eccentric, childlike, childish, wry, optimistic, intellectual, ironic, unhandy, forgetful, bad at math.*

You have your quirks, of course you do. Maybe it's not language with you, or bad math or memory, but I guarantee that there are ways you look at things that normal people do not. How do I know? Because otherwise what would draw you to standup? Sharing our bent perspective is the heart and soul of why we go up.

So write down your quirks. Start with the obvious ones – how friends find you funny – but then have a more thorough look around. Your comic filters are to be found in the unlikeliest corners of the person you are.

Once you have a robust list of your twists and traits – all these available comic filters – the next step is just to look at reality through the filters on that list. Pick any one you like, imagine that it's the *controlling idea of your brain*, and then explore how someone with that controlling idea would behave in any situation you can think of.

If you're *timid*, how do you cross the street or shop for food?

If your controlling idea is *madness*, how well do you do on a date?

If you're *claustrophobic*, how goes your elevator ride?

Armed with this information, you can now develop your material easily and with clear intent. Just take your strong comic filter, plug it into different situations and see what it does.

Nor are you limited to your own comic filters. Everyone you know, everyone you meet, everyone you *imagine* can filter reality for you in some funny way or another. Do you have an aging granddad (someone *my age*, yikes!) who's so out of touch with tech that he thinks Apple Pay is what you do at the fruit stand? If he's capable of that sort of cluelessness, why then he's capable of *any* sort of cluelessness, which means you don't just have a one-liner, you have a recurring character and a whole sustainable fountain of jokes. That's good news.

Here's more good news. Every comic filter you create is actually at least two filters: itself and its opposite. If there's *optimist* there's *pessimist*, if there's *footloose* there's *uptight*, and so on.

And when you start smashing opposite filters against each other, all sorts of interesting comic sparks start to fly. You're creating conflict and storing tension. You're also telling a story, the simple story of *A thinks X but B thinks Y and they fight.*

And it's all as easy as falling out of bed. Pick a character. *My imaginary friend Michael.* Assign that character a filter. *Macho.* Pick another character. *My imaginary friend Michaela.* Assign that character the opposite filter. *Feminista.*

Stick them in any situation – a hypothetical café, let us say – and find something for them to fight about. It can be anything. Sex, politics, coffee creamers. Whatever you pick, they're bound to fight because people with opposite filters *have* to fight. Maybe not like you and me, real people in the real world, but very much like people we enjoy making jokes about.

And how is it that these figments of your imagination or observation are not like you and me? It's a matter of **exaggeration**, another known and named comic tool. Exaggeration is what separates real reality from comic reality. It's Shakespeare's Falstaff being not just a fat, lazy coward, but the fattest, laziest coward in the world. It's Sam Kinison building his whole name and fame on his ability to elevate anger to howling rage. It's you, any time you find a filter that pleases you and then crank it up to eleven.

Try pushing some observations through a *wildly exaggerated* comic filter and see how that feels. For example, if you ever get a little bit annoyed by someone or something in your life, try jacking that annoyance up to the level of pure fury. You'll find (if you don't already know) that your material becomes livelier, more dynamic – funnier – when you take it to extremes.

Do you find it challenging to take things to extremes? Are you worried about going too far? Don't worry about that. You might think you're going too far, but really you're not. Why? Because the audience *wants* you to be extreme. They're not there to reason or be reasonable. They're there to laugh, and they're counting on you to deliver the goods by any means necessary. So if you find yourself censoring yourself – *they'll never let me get away with this* – try to push past that. It's better to have gone too far than never to have gone at all.

Take a comic filter and pin it to yourself. Create another character with the opposite filter. Milk the conflict. Surf the tension. Amp up the exaggeration. Go too far – way too far – and then just watch the walls of the club cave in. Revel in the vortex of chaos and uncontrollable laughter that you've created with your mere words. You don't get there by playing it safe. You get there by playing God, by using tools boldly, then more boldly still, and by ignoring anyone who says you shouldn't do this or you shouldn't do that.

We limit ourselves when we say, "I shouldn't," so that's something we likely shouldn't do.

RECAP

> - Use tools to support magic
> - Use comic filters to exploit situations strategically
> - Use exaggeration to create comic realities

5~ AWARENESS

What qualities or capabilities do you need to have in order to be successful in standup?

I can think of a few.

Sharp wit. Interesting ideas. Awesome agent. Sense of humor. Good work habits. Talent. Great material. People skills. Allies. Fans. Financial support. Drive and determination. Performance chops. Contacts. Moxie. A thick skin. A point of view. Attitude. Information. Perseverance. And so on.

All of these things *contribute* to the successful practice of standup. They're all part of the picture – but not the *main* part. Actually, the main part is something we've already touched on: awareness; specifically self-awareness – awareness of the self.

Without this awareness, your act can't grow because you can't shine a usefully critical light on your own work. With it, you're steadily ready to grow, and emotionally open to that growth.

The kind of awareness I'm talking about is not some sort of transcendence or enlightenment but just a simple and useful *feedback loop* that you can build in three easy steps.

1. Do a thing
2. Watch yourself doing it
3. Do it more

I write a joke and it doesn't work. I want it to work. I wish that it worked. I fear that it doesn't and, worse, that I can't fix it. In the name of giving myself useful feedback, I note these reactions, accept them, admit what I knew all along – yeah, the joke doesn't work – and then get into fixing it.

That's awareness in action.

Simple. Not mystical. A tool.

Take a moment now to give some of your older jokes a fresh, new look. Let go of the versions that currently exist and challenge yourself – just as an exercise – to break them down and build them back up. Or, if you prefer, crack the seal on some new material. Either way, watch yourself work. Notice how you do what you do. Be as aware of your **process** as you are aware of your **product**.

Once you acquire this habit of watching yourself work, you can start to make and store meaningful *process discoveries.* These discoveries in turn become handy, durable strategies that you can use over and over again, in service of your work, through your awareness feedback loop.

But only if you can step outside your ego.

I know this comic named Ariel Speedwagon (not her real name) (hell, not even a real person) who did this one set which killed this one time, and now she has invested all her faith and all her ego in it. To her it's not just a set anymore, it's a talisman – a lucky charm.

Only now her luck has run out, and no matter how hard she pushes the same jokes in the same way, she can never recapture that sublime lightning-in-a-bottle sensation she had that one time. At some point she will admit – if she is self-aware – that that one time was more of a fluke than a trend, and that creating material which consistently kills still awaits her progress and her hard work.

Without awareness, she can never let go, because the thing that she's chasing is just validation of previous success – a payoff on investment.

With awareness, she can seek to build an act that works now, in the present, even if that means tearing her old act down to the studs.

What she stands to lose is her sunk cost: all the time, skull sweat and ego she invested in the thing that she now has to let go.

What she stands to gain is a newer, better version of her work, driven by a deeper understanding of who she really is.

Awareness, then, is not a magical wonderland of insight – nirvana in Valhalla with a side of Velveeta – but just a gateway to growth.

If you practice awareness on these terms, you can expect many benefits...

> - Deeper understanding of yourself
> - Better understanding of your craft
> - Real insight into the world around you
> - Genuine empathy for other people
> - And some fricking funny jokes

With self-awareness, you can also expect to improve...

> - Your career prospects
> - Your relationships
> - Your level of contentment
> - Your ability to handle adversity
> - Your sense of self-worth

That's a ton, I mean a whole heaping pile of benefits. And what do we have to do to reap these rewards? Not much; just work. Put in the work. Because if we put in the work, then we are, by definition, *in our practice*.

And when you're in your practice – using insight to drive change – you are experiencing legitimate personal growth, and that growth applies to each and every aspect of who you are and who you want to become – onstage, offstage, all around the town.

I'm going to ask you to do an exercise – and *really do it*, okay? This exercise will challenge you to think about yourself from the inside out. You might find the prospect daunting; it can be hard to self-confront. But remember, change is growth. It's okay to put yourself on the line.

First, write down a list of things about yourself that you don't want anyone to know. Make it a long list. Really dredge it all up. Don't worry, I won't make you share.

Next, try and turn those secrets into jokes. Oops, sorry, guess I want you to share after all.

But it's good for you. Really, it is. For one thing, once your secrets are out there, you no longer have to worry about everyone finding them out, and that's a big load off of anyone's mind. For another thing – a thing I know you know – material that looks inside is richer, more heartfelt, just altogether more *worthy* than material that looks almost anywhere else.

I'm sure it hasn't escaped your attention that some of the best standup comics share their secrets openly and bravely – brazenly, almost. I'm thinking of Richard Pryor and Marc Maron. I'm thinking of Kevin Hart and Tig Notaro. I'm thinking of every comic I met while researching my documentary *Misery Loves Comedy*.

I'm thinking of you. Right now, I am thinking of you and the fear you face in moving away from surface observations and down into the stuff that really matters – away from, let us say, "My Uber driver has an unpronounceable name," all the way down to "I steal my friends' drugs."

And I'm thinking of me, thinking about how I know a sure-fire cure for hemorrhoids, but how can I share that secret without looking like, you know, a guy with hemorrhoids?

Your fears are part of your voice. Hard things to speak of are part of your voice. Your secrets are a source of your richest material. Mine them for jokes. If it's all too raw or too painful for you to share yet, that's okay – you truly don't have to share. But what you'll be practicing is how to develop material that's hard to develop – emotionally hard – and this will be useful to you in the long run, whether anyone ever sees these particular efforts or not.

RECAP

- ➤ Use awareness feedback loops
- ➤ Use your insights to drive change
- ➤ Material that's hard to share is worth sharing

6~ AUDIENCE

When you watch other comics take the stage, what do you think they're really after? Maybe they want to slay the crowd – just kill. Or gain approval. Prove a point. Process their shit. Make bank. Get a laugh. Get laid. Whatever. People get into standup for all kinds of reasons, of course.

It's useful to know yours.

So take a moment now and ask yourself what you hope to achieve with that mighty comic voice of yours. Do you seek to please or displease? Foster outrage? Promote understanding? Tickle every funny bone you can? *What do you want?* Or even what *many* things do you want? It's always fine to have more than one goal; many a standup comic wants to get both paid *and* laid.

Right now, with this mighty comic voice of mine, what I want is to amuse and uplift. I really want to tickle those funny bones; however, more broadly, I really want to add joy to the world.

I mean this sincerely. It's not a setup to some punchline. It's my sense of higher purpose. I don't know for sure that a standup comic *needs* a higher purpose, but I do know that mine serves me every day, just by lending clarity to my decisions and inspiring me to energetic efforts. It's self-evident, if you think about it: How could I ever add joy to the world if I didn't even know that was my goal?

Gotta know your goal.

Here are the goals of some imaginary standups I know. Mopey Moperson wants to be a buzzkill. Scopey Scoperson wants to speak truth to power. Hopey Hoperson wants to make a living.

And Ropey Roperson wants to be a cowboy. Well, there you go, different strokes for different folks.

What about you? Why are you here where you are? Give it some thought. Jot down those thoughts. Maybe you'll arrive at something as simple as this: *I want to win friends and influence people.*

"Okay," you agreeably agree, "I want to win friends and influence people. That's my goal. So what's my next step?"

Your next step is to think about the audience and what *they* want.

Oh, it's a given that different audiences want different things. Little kids want poo jokes. Frat boys want screw jokes. Cobblers want shoe jokes. But at the end of the day they all just want the same thing:

good laughs. And you get to deliver those laughs, winning over your audience one joke at a time.

But remember, there's never been a comedian in the history of comedy who was universally adored. In every audience, there are some people you can't win over – or even decently entertain – just because they don't agree with your premise or point of view, or because they don't get what you're driving at, or they've heard your jokes before, or they plain don't care.

You can't please all the people all the time; this is not news. However, what you *can* do is think of your audience as a bell curve. You're always going to lose the ends of the curve to people who are too smart or too dumb or too invested or too distracted to pick up what you're putting down. Let 'em go, and set your sights instead on this: the bell curve's Big Fat Middle, or BFM.

The BFM is the audience you're after – the majority of people who are inclined to listen to you or even who just find themselves listening to you. To capture them, consider the things that concern them – not all of them but most of them. Sex, religion, politics, life, death, football, *futbol*, fast food, fast times or fast cash. Write up a **topic list** of the major and minor involvements in your listeners' lives.

Once you have this list, you can start to gain real insight into your audience and start linking that insight to laughs – which you can do just by looking at your BFM's interests through your own strong comic filter.

This approach does a couple of good things. First, it ensures that your act is about something that's at least *of interest* to your audience. Second, it gets you outside your own head. While it's great to talk about things that concern you – what you're passionate about and dying to get into – this can be a self-indulgence. Some comics are completely self-indulgent. I'm sure you know a few; I could mention one I know, *Selfindulgey Selfindulgerson,* but that would be the worst sort of self-indulgence, so I won't.

The thing is, as long as you're talking about something congruent to your audience's interests, it will *never* be a self-indulgence, because they'll be right there with you – interested. This is not about pandering to them, surrendering to their expectations or changing your viewpoint to suit them. It's just about taking them into account. The more you know what compels your audience's attention, the more in tune with them you can become. To gain this insight, just ask two questions:

- ➢ Who is my tribe?
- ➢ What is their anxiety?

(This is received wisdom, by the way, from my screenwriting sensei, Paul Thompson of New York

University.) (Thanks, Godfather.) (Also, let's not get hung up on the word "tribe" here, which can mean different things to different people. For our purposes, your tribes are just your affinity groups – people to whom you feel connected across common interests, objectives, background, region, vocation, culture, beliefs, feelings, hobbies, habits and so on.)

As it turns out, your tribe is actually many different tribes. I am a writer, an artist, a married man, a dog owner, a poker player, an ultimate player, a baby boomer, a chrome dome, an obsessive collector, a Californian, an American, a human and more, and anyone with whom I share any of these characteristics is in one or another of my tribes.

Armed with this information, I can now ask...

> ➢ Who is my tribe? *Dog owners*
> ➢ What is their anxiety? *Picking up poop*

... and I can build a bit around an epic plastic bag fail.

Or even something funny.

You can do the same, over and over, again and again, gaining new insight into your audience and what makes them tick. Give it a go. Think about (and write down) the interests, irritations, hopes, dreams, fears, concerns or other self-identifications that you and your audience share. That'll give you plenty to work with right there.

Okay, fine, but what do we do with tribes that aren't *our* tribes? Like, I could get booked to do a show at a Humvee drivers' convention, and I don't know the first thing about Humvees. I don't even think they're a particularly good idea, but I can see why people like them. And I can easily guess those people's anxieties: high fuel prices... low public approval... parking problems...

Hey, parking problems! Now that's an anxiety I share, because while I don't drive a Humvee, I do drive and I do park. Now I can write a joke that creates a bridge to this tribe: *If the universe is constantly expanding, why can't I find a place to park?*

I know this isn't the very best joke ever written (I have that joke saved in another folder), but it's one that I arrived at by finding issues or concerns that I and my audience share. If you take this approach, you're going to build a reliable and renewable way to generate topics, explore rich sources of material, connect with your audience and write jokes that matter – to them *and* to you.

RECAP

> ➢ Know what you want
> ➢ Know what your audience wants
> ➢ Write jokes where those sets intersect

7~ THE HOPE MACHINE

This shit is hard. Every day it's hard. Finding the time, making the time, squeezing out the time to work on our craft, that's hard.

Standing up to skepticism and staring down the doubts of family and friends? Hard.

Living up to the promises we've made to ourselves and meeting the goals we've set for ourselves... hard, hard.

And then doing what we do, writing and rewriting our jokes – God, getting notes on them – then signing up for our mics and rising up through the ranks to road warrior, featured performer, back room regular, front room headliner, Netflix-special or sitcom maker and beyond, it's all hard.

But what lies ahead is the crazy rocket ship ride to superstardom, right? And then, at last, all the hard work will be behind us, right? Right?

Not quite.

I can remember thinking along those lines when I first got to Hollywood. I figured that after I knocked out a couple of scripts, the world would take note and lavish me with fame and praise, and then I would become this "made guy" and I would never have to hustle for gigs again. I was wrong. I've always been wrong. Despite much success, the need to hustle never went away.

Still hasn't. It's still right here, staring me in the face, even as I write these words.

Why?

Because *gap*.

Because there's always a gap between where we are and where we want to be, and that gap doesn't magically vanish when we pass certain thresholds of achievement or acclaim.

But this is okay. This just means that growth doesn't stop once we get big, if we get big.

Also growth doesn't stop even if we don't get big.

Why?

Because *hope*.

Because the same urge that drives us to write and tell jokes drives us also to never stop trying to make it all pay off.

To me, hope looks like a slot machine; I call it the hope machine. Every time I chase an opportunity, I can feel myself giving that handle a tug. Tug, tug, tug, hoping that this time the reels will align. Of course I want the big jackpot, but I'm not picky. I'll take any paid work if it advances my craft. There's growth there, and I'm content to invest in my growth.

Are you drawn to fame? Does it shine like a light on your horizon, beckoning you into your future? That's great, that's fine; set lofty goals and set sail. Enjoy the ride! But don't forget the main thing, and that's to build a *sustainable practice*. Day in and day out, count on yourself to come through for yourself. That's how you get locked into the practical habit of striving toward standup.

Once you're locked in, you don't give a second thought to putting in the work. You're a fish in water, and good daily work habits become second nature. If you're in that place already, great, keep doing what you're doing. If you're not there yet, maybe go at it like a game – this game that I'm making up right now, but also that Ralphie May made up long ago, as have countless other comics before and since.

My version of the game is called *Score Points to Advance*, and it's simple to play: just score points to advance.

> - points for writing your first set
> - points for going up

- ➤ points for going up cold
- ➤ points for retooling your act
- ➤ points for pwning a heckler
- ➤ points for landing a "reach" gig
- ➤ points for getting paid

What other points can you score? List them. Try to score them. If you score enough points, you get, I don't know… a cheesecake, if you like cheesecake.

Actually what you really get is just the chance to score most points. You get to stay in the game. Working hard – seeing yourself accomplish things – gives you all the faith you need to stay in the game.

Well, that's all well and good, but can faith realistically be warranted here? After all, not everyone ends up on the crazy rocket ship ride to superstardom. That's true, but still faith is always warranted, not as pie-in-the-sky stuff but just as the fuel we use; our propellant. It pushes us past obstacles. Drives us to put in the work. Helps us get back up when we get knocked down.

Faith tells us what we want our future to look like and then empowers us to create it.

Before I was locked into my practice, I invested my faith in many things, for the specific sake of sustaining myself. I had my faith in my writing ability, sense of humor and sticktoitiveness, and faith that people would find their way to my work. And I had faith in the life-changing phone call; I just *knew* that good news lay ahead.

What do you have faith in? Who do you want to become? You may not be used to asking yourself such questions — or maybe you ask them all the time. Either way, let's take a moment here to paint a mental picture of our future. Couldn't hurt. Might help us clarify our path. I'll go first. What do I really want my future to hold?

I guess in a word I'd say "more." More years, of course, but also more opportunity. More words and more art. More jokes. More books written. More audiences reached. More clients served. More service in general. That's what I want my future to look like.

How about you? If your picture comes clear to you, that's terrific: You've found a point in your future that you can pull yourself toward.

If your picture does not come clear, if you find that you just can't think concretely about the road ahead, it may be that a certain sort of fear is clouding your vision: the fear of **bad outcomes**.

Any time we tackle anything, we have a fear of bad outcomes. In big ways and small, we're always thinking, "What's the worst that can happen?" and then painting a vivid and troubling picture of that.

Maybe that's just me. I know that my brain doesn't work like others', so maybe these fears that vex me don't vex you at all. But one of my goals for this book is to reveal and share my process, so if you want to see how I get vexed, let me show you what that looks like:

I'm on a stage somewhere when I think of a new joke, and I think I might tell it, but before I can even form the words, I hear a little voice inside my head, a voice I long ago identified as my Ferocious Editor. And my Ferocious Editor says, "Hang on JV, don't tell that joke just yet because it might not be funny and if it's not funny, they won't laugh, and if they don't laugh they won't like you, and if they don't like you, you can't like yourself, and if you can't like yourself, then you must experience full-on ego death and pass away..."

Man, that's a lot of pressure to put on a joke, especially one that *I haven't even told yet!* Yet pressure persists and fear persists, and this fear is a major block to my growth if it keeps me from seizing opportunities, even the modest opportunity of trying out a new joke.

Is any of this going on in your head?

- ➢ *If I sign up for this mic, I will bomb*
- ➢ *If I try to write this sketch, it will suck*
- ➢ *If I joke about my family, they'll kill me*
- ➢ *If I commit to this future, I'll fail*
- ➢ *If I claim to be "worthy" in any sense, I'll be mercilessly mocked and deservedly so*

Those are fears, fears of bad outcomes. I'm sure you can name others that you know. To defeat them all, just do this: *don't fear bad outcomes.*

Easier said than done? Not at all. Easily done exactly as said. "Don't fear bad outcomes." Just don't fear 'em.

I knew this standup comic once – not me but one Schmon Schmorhaus – who served his jokes up to his audience on a platter of insecurity. His mentality was all, *please like my jokes and please don't hate me!* He desperately needed his audience's approval and feared he could not win it. As a result, he could never deliver the best version of his material because he was always too uptight.

The situation improved when he stopped fearing bad outcomes. That gave him the courage – permission, really – to try any joke or chase any chance. He knew that the worst thing that could happen to him was a bad outcome – but he trained himself not to care about those. He never silenced his Ferocious Editor, but he gained the upper hand.

This is a big idea, just huge.

When you genuinely don't fear bad outcomes, you can tackle any project, take any risk. You can break old habits. Carve out time for your practice. Tell bold and daring jokes. Go up on scary stages. Why?

Because the worst that can happen is a bad outcome – and bad outcomes don't matter to you.

If you want to have the direct experience of not fearing bad outcomes, here are three tricks you can use.

Do the new. When I'm feeling like my creativity needs shaking up, I just challenge myself to do something, anything, that I've never done before. Doesn't matter what. Brush my teeth with the wrong hand, run naked through a cornfield, write ten jokes about the common cockchafer (look it up). I'm going to do the new because I know that when I do, I will get unexpected outcomes – and there's no way I can fear those because *I don't even know what they'll be.* This lets me experience things without judging them, and helps me understand that, yes, I actually can find a way to not fear bad outcomes.

If you play this game, you can expect to pass through predictable stages. At first you might feel nervous, uncertain, for you'll be stepping outside your norms, outside your comfort zone. Soon, though, you'll start to feel powerful, as you experience the jolt of outlaw energy you get when you start breaking old rules. Finally, you will feel just high – high on your power to make interesting things happen simply by entering the unknown. Also, probably, you will laugh. I don't know why, it's just that the new thing is always funny somehow. Well, try it – you'll soon see for yourself.

Try to fail. Sometimes I want to have good ideas, but I get so fretful that my ideas are bad, or likely to be judged bad, that I'm blocked from having any ideas at all. To bust that block, I stop trying to come up with any good ideas and purposefully go looking for bad ones instead. The beauty of this strategy is *I just can't lose.* If I succeed in having a bad idea, I've met my goal, and that's a win, right? But if I have an idea that turns out to be really not so bad, then I'm ahead of the game in a different way, because now I have an idea – a joke, a bit, a story – that I can actually use. When you deliberately make it your goal to have bad outcomes, you'll find that it's hard to fear them at all.

Maybe you recognize this as a useful fiction – *I'm gonna suck on purpose! Wait and see if I don't!* Okay, that just means that your process is working as it should. When you see yourself tricking yourself, the important thing is that *you're seeing yourself.* You might even be manipulating yourself, but that, too, is okay, since your goal is a worthy one: more jokes and better performance by you.

Have more outcomes. Those of you who have read *The Comic Toolbox* will know the Rule of Nine, which says, "for every ten jokes we try, nine won't work." That looks like bad math and bad news, but really it's not, because once you recognize that – just in the nature of things – many, many, many jokes won't work, then you can write lots of jokes without fear, and you don't have to invest much ego in any one of them. Pile up your outcomes. Keep piling them up until the fear of bad outcomes just gets lost in the noise.

This is why some standups go up and up and up – five, ten, a dozen mics a week – so that any given failure can simply get lost in the noise. If you're the sort of standup who has trouble going up, the solution, really, is just to start going up lots more, more than you're used to or even feel comfortable with. Put in enough repetitions and you'll soon stop fearing the bad outcome of any one set. And if you think they'll *all* be bad, well, I'm sorry, but you're just wrong.

One last thing in this chapter, and that's the story of me and my lifelong love for the sport of ultimate frisbee. After four decades of devoted play, I blew out my right shoulder and had to learn to throw left-handed. It was terrible, humiliating; I looked like a spaz. But I've looked like a spaz before. It's just a bad outcome and I don't fear those.

So I kept practicing my terrible, humiliating throws until eventually they started to be less terrible. These days I have a decent lefty. It's not going to win any prizes, but I get to keep playing ultimate, and to me that matters a lot. I pushed through the bad to get to the good, which – even in the face of the world's worst outcomes – is something we can always strive to do.

RECAP

> ➢ Invest your faith in your future
> ➢ Use strategies to empower yourself
> ➢ Stop fearing bad outcomes by welcoming them instead

8~ STATUS

For comics in the company of other comics, it's common to contemplate status. Who are you above? Who's above you? Where does the power lie? Who makes the decisions?

And what else? What other thoughts – worries, obsessions – cross your mind when you find yourself in the collaborative/competitive hothouse of a standup comedy show? Also, how do you feel when you're there? A lot of standups feel crappy just then. They imagine their status to be lower than anyone's, or threatened by everyone. Onstage and offstage, they feel like their fate is not in their hands.

Some try to solve this problem by **upbonding**, attaching themselves to peers with perceived higher status. This doesn't really do the trick, though, because while they're moving in higher circles, they still don't feel like they belong. That was me for sure as a low-stakes poker player rubbing shoulders with high-roller celebrities; if anything, I felt like a mascot.

Others fend off status self-consciousness by **overgiving**. This can work. If you're running a mic, promoting a show, doing your part, you feel a sense of belonging and you get to hitch a ride on the group's higher status. That's a healthy way to participate in a standup community or any community, but it can still leave your feelings toward status unresolved.

I'd like it better if status didn't matter. I'd like it better if I could ignore all the questions of who's higher and who's lower, and just do my own thing, without measuring myself against anyone or having them measure themselves against me.

To achieve this, I'm going to do two things: lift status by changing goals, and level status by making common cause.

Lift status by changing goals. The brutal truth is that low status sucks – and low-status conditions abound in the life of a striving standup. You know what I'm talking about. Any time you're asking for a spot, or a better spot, or money, permission, promotion, approval, anything, you're pushing uphill against status. Why? Because low status lives in any situation where *you want to get* what *they have the power to give*. If you want a job (or validation), and they have a job (or validation) on offer, you're in low status looking up.

And low status sucks! It makes us feel ineffective, inferior, powerless – literally without power. In that funked-up frame of mind it's hard to do anything well, especially important things like our act. It's a bad situation, and the bad situation reliably gets worse if we then put more pressure on ourselves — which we're likely to do when status is low. It's the old *If I bomb, I die!* fearadigm, exacerbated by low status and this sense of need to get something — anything — from bookers, agents, critics, audience or even just peers.

But we already know how to deal with this: don't fear bad outcomes.

They might have status over you, but they can't make you fear bad outcomes, and if you're not fearing bad outcomes then you're just there having fun. Onstage or anywhere, when you shift your goal to ***just have fun*** you reduce the pressure you put on yourself, which can only upgrade your efforts. Plus, when you don't fear bad outcomes, you feel like you have nothing to lose, and this puts you outside of status altogether, because status is only ever an issue when people feel like they have something to lose.

Level status by making common cause. Status is out of balance in any sort of *we're buying/they're selling* situation. To create balance, we just need to redefine our terms. Instead of *you're selling/I'm buying*, try to think and speak in terms of *how can I contribute to common goals?*

It makes a difference — all the difference in the world. When you enter an audition, a negotiation or an interview informed by the idea that you have something to contribute, several really good things happen. Your sense of self-worth goes up because you see yourself injecting real value into the equation. This makes stress go down, which helps improve execution. Plus, focusing on common goals makes you literally less self-conscious – less conscious of the self – which naturally helps you feel more at ease.

Wow, that sounds like a party with candles and cake for you – and all you have to do to host it is change your outlook from *I need but you have* to *we both need and we both have.* This will feel better in your head and also yield better outcomes.

Consider this imaginary audition. Watch how status is addressed, leveled and gently set aside...

Spicy actress Penny Arrabiata goes to an audition feeling like she really has to crush it or it's curtains for her career. Well, that's pressure, and if that pressure is left unaddressed, it's bound to hurt her performance. So she rethinks her goal for the audition, changing it from *book this role or die!* to *let's just have us some fun.* Having fun, that's something she can do.

Penny sails through the audition, having fun – no stakes, no pressure, no problem. The casting director starts having fun, too, because at last here's one performer who's not so uptight as the rest. And these two people are already making common cause, just through the act of sharing a good moment, which is a little win for them both.

Now all Penny has to do is identify joint objectives and offer to do her part. When she does this, a certain kind of alchemy takes place: Her offer to contribute actually affirms the idea that she has something to contribute. That's big. It's kinda the key to the whole thing. Status becomes level at the exact moment when you validate yourself, which you can do pretty much just by doing it.

Does it worry you that you can't validate yourself because you don't have enough value – or even any – to throw into the mix? But you already have plenty! Apart from your own talent, humor, jokes, knowledge, good looks and native intelligence, you can always contribute such universal positive qualities as dedication, reliability, empathy, creativity, enthusiasm and good spirit. You say that you lack experience? No problem. Contribute your energy instead. You don't need experience to have energy, right?

So there's always a contribution to be made. And when you make that contribution, your status woes vanish because you have told yourself and everyone else that you're not trapped in ego, you have your mind on higher things. You might think this would make you come across as arrogant, but in fact when you're serving common cause, you always come across as humble. Plus thoughtful, insightful, self-aware, generous and more. That's the kind of person most of us want to be, and most of us like to be with.

Once you get the hang of lifting and leveling status, you can operate more effectively in any realm, but especially in the fraught and overwrought realm of standup. Just in the matter of going up, you can now stop mentally apologizing for yourself or your set and instead simply go ahead and make your meaningful contribution to a successful show.

Not only is that a better place to be professionally, it's much healthier emotionally. Your commitment to balanced status is also a tangible commitment to yourself: your autonomy, agency, freedom, power, dignity and vision. These are all qualities that you want to protect, and you can protect them just by making it clear that you always bring value when you come.

To put it another way, no one pushes you around when you're serving common cause. Take pride in your craft and let them know that you do. That's a sturdy platform to stand on in most situations.

Of course, as you know, status isn't always low. Sometimes it's high – like when you're onstage and you're killing it. When could status possibly be higher than when you have them eating out of the palm of your hand, literally looking up to you and bathing you in approval? So the question's worth asking: What should we do with status when status is high?

Answer: Shed it. Dump it.

Use it to lift others up.

Do it as fast as you can.

This might seem counterintuitive, like, *if I have all this status, why on earth would I want to give it away?* Here's why: because your audience came to have fun, and they'll have more fun if you make them equal partners in their own good time. I mean, they are, are they not? You can't do your job without them. When you let them know you know this, status is leveled, and now they're relaxed and ready to let you take them anywhere you want to go.

Yet you might still hold onto an ego construct along the lines of, "It's my show, my time, and everyone should shut up and listen to me!" If I'm in your audience, I'm going to have a hard time having fun with that. You can't order me into your world, but you might try inviting me in.

When I come willingly, I feel empowered. I am grateful to you for empowering me, and I reward you with laughs.

I have a friend who did tons of Zoom standup during the pandemic. I won't tell you her name – let's call her Smashley Shmutermuth. She says she always invited her viewers to turn on their video and unmute their mics. It made them feel welcome and connected — more at home, weirdly, in their own homes. She got them primed for a good time, which made it easier to deliver one, even under the challenges of Zoom.

Me, I've spent a lot of time running writers' rooms with lots of insecure writers. I've had all the status — I was their boss. But I spread that status around. I did everything I could to create common cause. It was just in my interest. When I lifted their status I reduced their anxiety and therefore improved their performance. The better they performed, of course, the less work I had to do. Wasn't that a win for me? Wasn't it a win for them?

Now here comes a secret, an important one: Every time you think you're yielding or shedding status, you're actually raising yours up. In empowering others (this is gonna get meta so stay with me) you're flexing the power to empower. You have power; otherwise you couldn't empower. And who has power? Someone with high status. In fact and in practice, the more status you share, the more you will gain.

Reminds me of a joke about the enterprising sex worker who said of their economic model, "Is this a great business or what? You got it, you sell it, you still got it!"

Empower your audience. They won't heckle you, they'll l-o-v-e love you.

Empower fellow standups. When they win and they know you helped them win, you get a piece of the win. I'm not talking about money but about the psychic income you earn whenever you help others succeed.

Empower the future. For those following behind you on your path – younger maybe, less polished perhaps – give them support. They already see you as better, more experienced, but now you're also this cool person who helps starter-outers and follow-alongers. Man, you can dine out on that positive vibe all your life. And I say that as someone who, I'm here to tell you, definitely has.

RECAP

- Get a handle on status
- Own your value
- Empower the crap out of everyone

9~ STUCK

There comes a time in everyone's standup practice when they just... stall... out. This can be when the joke well runs dry, or when they hit a booking ceiling they can't break through. Or maybe it's writer's block, or just an everyday case of the blues. What should you do if it happens to you? First, don't be surprised. Like I said, it happens to everyone, and you're part of everyone, so, yeah, it's gonna happen to you. Second, know that it will pass because things change. Things always change.

Sometimes quicker than you think.

You have your day in the sun and you think to yourself, "At last I have arrived!" That's how I felt the first time I put on my *Charles in Charge* staff writer jacket. Little did I know that I would be fired from that job the following week.

You have a setback and it seems like the end of the world. That's how I felt when my Hollywood career bottomed out. Little did I know that I was about to sell my first how-to book and start my exciting new career as a professional expert.

You're in a funk or a fog that just won't lift. That's how I felt when I found myself writing novels that I couldn't sell. Little did I know that I was about to discover digital art and completely transform my practice.

Little do we realize how much change is packed into the package of life. I never knew this when I was young, and it vexed me terribly, but I eventually came to terms with it.

Which may be cold comfort to you right now if you feel like you're going nowhere fast.

So what can we do, now, today, to unstick the stuck parts? Here are some strategies I use. Borrow these or develop your own.

Be honest. Be honest about your material. Is it really as strong as you think it is, or have you just become used to it and comfortable delivering it? Maybe those jokes have worn out their welcome or lost their edge over time. Maybe you're tired of telling them. Maybe they're just *old.* Whatever; it's always a good idea to refresh your set, but never more so than when you feel blocked by forces beyond your control, because refreshing your set is something that you *can* control, so it just makes sense to invest your energy there.

Make a marketing push. Can I be honest with you? I hate marketing like a cat hates baths. When work is coming my way, I never invest five minutes in promoting myself. But when the work slows down, *I don't slow down.* In my professional life, I'm always either executing my projects or hustling for new ones. If you, too, rate marketing as ten out of ten on the cat-bath annoyance scale, I hear ya! But when you're stuck you can easily get unstuck just by putting yourself out there. Remember, DFBO – don't fear bad outcomes. This will set you free to climb in the bath with the cat.

Give yourself a break. Your long-term success will depend on your ability to drive yourself forward without driving yourself bonkers – so mental healthfulness matters. If things are not going well, just take a break. Step away from the work and gain some perspective. Recharge your batteries. Then return to your craft with diligence and full commitment to your goals. I promise, you'll come back stronger every time.

Seek small wins. If big wins are eluding you, rack up some smaller ones. This will build both your confidence and your expertise, and set you up for the bigger wins you crave. I did it just now when I reached out to a certain podcast that I want to be a guest on. That was a win. It's true: Whether they end up booking me or not, *just reaching out* is a win. And don't think that I have an advantage because I'm "that *Comic Toolbox* guy." There are small wins all around you all the time, and you can have as many as you want, just by going after them. Of course this contributes to your practice and your craft, but mainly it just makes you feel good and gets you out of your funk, so yay.

Grab an ally. There you are in a leaky boat on a still and silent sea. Look around. Is there someone in your same boat? Can you help each other out? Maybe write some jokes together, or give and get notes on your sets. Even just talk each other up. As you already know, contributing to the success of others is a great way to peel off some success for yourself. And remember, a rising tide lifts all boats – even the lonely, leaky ones.

Grab more allies. Standup comedy is a collective form of art; it works best when there's lots of people involved. Just on that basis alone, you're going to need the collaborative company of others; however, never is this need greater than when things are not going well. That's why it's always good practice to find, join, support, build or otherwise grow your own little standup nation. Lean on them when you need help, and be there for them when they do. "Comedy is community," says the sage, and we here all agree.

Be honest. I'm repeating this one because it bears repeating: If things aren't going your way, there must be something – some small or large thing – that you can do to change things for the better. But this will only happen if you're truthful enough to see and patch the holes in your game. They are exactly where you expect to find them: hiding behind ego; hiding from fear. A frank appraisal of where you are now is the first step toward moving forward from there.

Be more self-aware. If you're stuck – really stuck – if you're genuinely working hard and not improving, it could be that your level of self-awareness needs a boost. But awareness is easily distracted. We get caught up in the drama around us because it's often easier to deal with the drama than to face certain facts of our practice. Don't be distracted by drama. Don't be dissuaded by fear. Be the person you are and accept the person you are. The more deeply you know and accept yourself, the better your comedy... and your process... and your life... will be.

Hey, you know what? I mentioned writer's block a few pages back, and it now occurs to me that you might like to know how to end writer's block forever. I happen to have the key to that elusive mystery right here...

What should you do as a joke writer or any kind of writer when writer's block strikes? The simple and surprising answer is: just don't write.

Wait, what? Don't write? That makes no sense. How can not-writing possibly solve the problem of not writing? Isn't not-writing exactly the issue? What the hell has JV been smoking?

JV has been smoking nothing. JV knows that writer's block takes place at the specific intersection of too much fear and too little information. Let's break it down.

Too much fear. When faced with a difficult writing problem, like, say, coming up with a great button for a bit, the feeling may naturally creep in that, oops, this is a problem we can't actually solve. This feeling quickly drives us to the brink of creative insecurity and leaves us staring into the void. Now we start to feel a weight of dread draped around our necks: *This writer's block is never going to end!* And this stops us cold because how we can write anything good or funny when we're consumed with such self-doubt? The creative self looks at itself and says, "Yikes! I truly suck!" This initiates an insidious negative feedback loop, where we see ourselves failing creatively, which undermines our confidence, and then, lacking confidence, we just go ahead and fail some more. Now we're really in crisis – a crisis of fear.

And that's what writer's block really is: not the absence of words but the presence of fear. You've pulled a metaphorical muscle – your creative muscle – and now that muscle is in spasm: temporarily broken, temporarily scared, temporarily no damn good.

Too little information. Interestingly, the thing that triggers this vicious cycle is usually just not knowing enough about the problem we're trying to solve. We haven't sufficiently stoked our mental engines with the right kind of fuel. Maybe we need more research about the facts of our bit. Maybe we need to deepen our understanding of our comic filter or controlling idea. Maybe we just need to broaden our search – let new information seep in. Or maybe we need to go deeper into ourselves, and figure out what the heck we're really trying to say. Whatever information we're lacking, it's the *lack of information* that has put us where we are. If you don't believe me, just ask yourself what you'd be doing if you did have enough information to write your jokes. That's right, you'd be writing your jokes. Without fear and without doubt, you would be in creative command.

When you're not in command, that's when you stand at the intersection of too much fear and too little information. And that's when you get to take the radical advice of: *if you can't write, stop trying.* Just stop. Put down your pen. Walk away from the keyboard. Go do something else instead – and that specific something else is this: gather information.

Gathering information is a left-brain function. (I can never remember which side of the brain does what, so I use this handy mnemonic: "left is for logic, right is for rock 'n' roll.") During writer's block, the right side of the brain just isn't working, and it feels so sad. But the left side, the logic side, is working just fine. You may doubt that you'll ever write another joke, but you don't doubt that you can look shit up. That's easy-peasy, right? So that's what we'll do here. We'll look shit up. We'll never feel fear doing research because research – gathering information – is something that the left brain does effortlessly well. When you're gathering information, your ego is never threatened or even engaged.

Therefore, when writing is hard but harvesting data is easy, don't do the hard thing, do the easy thing instead.

Now watch what happens. Over here, your left brain is gathering information. Because this is easy, you start to relax and that terrible creative cramping starts to subside. Fear diminishes. The overwhelming paralytic feeling of *I suck forever!* fades away, ignored by a left brain that's focused on something it does easily and well. The right brain comes out of crisis, looks around, and what does it find? Lots of interesting new information to work with!

Before you know it, both informed and excited by all the new connections and discoveries you've made, you find yourself writing again. Simply, efficiently, effectively, automatically. And all because you made the decision not to write when writing was hard to do.

Let's make it step-by-step, shall we?

1/ Recognize that you are writer's-blocked. How will you know? Duh, you're not writing.

2/ Stop trying to force your way past the block, as that will just yield yucky results and make you feel worse.

3/ Go gather some information. Look both outside and inside yourself; sometimes the answers are already in your head, you just need to study them more closely.

4/ Relax your brain. When you're doing research your ego will stop tormenting you because, hey, any ol' ego can do research.

5/ Find yourself back writing again, huzzah!

6/ Repeat as necessary. And it will be necessary, alas; new writing problems always lie ahead.

So there you go. Writer's block solved and sorted, forever and ever, amen. Don't thank me, I define myself through service.

RECAP

- Use tools and strategies to get unstuck
- Be honest with yourself and engaged with others
- Sneakily cure writer's block by not writing

10~ LET'S BUILD A BIT

Let's build a bit. We'll use a strategy that comes to us out of storytelling, where a story is often understood in its simplest terms as *a pivot from rejection to acceptance of a proposition or situation.* Using this approach we can wed comedy to narrative drive and use the power of story to energize our jokes.

Let's say we want to do something with Adam and Eve in the Garden of Eden. We can always hit it with stand-alone jokes – *"Stand back! I don't know how big this thing's gonna get!"* – but how can we build a legitimate bit, something with somewhere to go?

Start with an attitude. There they are in the Garden of Eden, Adam and Eve, not eating the apple. There they are, resisting temptation. Their *attitude* is one of *rejection.* Specifically, they're rejecting the idea that eating the apple is a good idea.

Now along comes the serpent bringing the *pivot*, which is – hang on, it's a mouthful – *a new piece of information that triggers a change in emotional state.* When the snake is all, "Apples! Yum!" that's the pivot, and next thing you know our heroes are tempted — impacted by new information — and fallen, alas. They've made the emotional pivot from rejection to acceptance.

This bit, then, has three parts: rejection, pivot, acceptance. To slot your jokes into this structure, just ask what attitude fits the part of the story you're in.

During *rejection*, Adam and Eve are fighting their urges, so you can talk about how hard it is to not eat a damn apple or how hard to pretend they don't care, or anything else that reflects their current emotional state: *Apples? Bah!*

With the *pivot* and the new information, Adam and Eve are transformed. In this part of the bit, you can drive the comedy through the perspective of the catalyzing character — in this case, that wily serpent — and also through the couple's emotional uncertainty about their brave new world. *Apples? Hmm...*

In *acceptance*, you just see where they're at. Are Adam and Eve defeated or proud, meek or rebellious? Enslaved or free? Who have you helped them become? *Apples? Yay!*

Now all that's left is to button the bit: *And God said, with a considerable amount of reverb, "You don't have to go home but you can't stay here-ere-ere!"*

So that's beginning, middle and end of a bit. For a button, we can add a *twist*, where we take a previously established attitude and turn it inside out.

Maybe it turns out that God and the snake were in cahoots all along, and they just wanted Eden all to themselves.

Using this formula, you can build a bit on any subject you can think of, just by asking three simple questions:

How does this start out?

What makes it change?

What does it become?

Answering those questions will breathe life into any topic you choose, because now you're moving your comedy away from just *watching things unfold* and into *moving the narrative along.*

Say you want to write a bit about supermarket checkout lines. Nothing wrong with that topic. It's been done before, but not by you, so, yeah, let's give it a go.

There you are in the supermarket line. The people in front of you are *so... damn... slow.* What's your attitude? How do you feel? Me, I'm feeling impatient, like, *I'm falling behind in my existence!*

For this supermarket checkout line or any other moment you're in, if you are in any sense feeling unhappy – bored, angry, stressed, vexed, peeved – you can be said to be *in rejection of circumstance.* In this part of the bit, your jokes are all about *when will this* (comically exaggerated) *nightmare end?*

Now comes the pivot, the new piece of information that triggers the change in emotional state. Anything will do here. Anything that you observe or imagine can be used to flip the switch.

Like maybe you're distracted by an attractive person of the opposite sex or the same sex. Or maybe a cute child catches your eye. Or the person in line behind you has nothing in their cart but tuna and gin and *what's up with that, a party for them and their cat?* When you shift your attention away from your bad mood and to, well, anything else at all, that's when you propel yourself into your new emotional state.

Me, here in the supermarket of my mind, I choose to scan the magazine racks, and soon enough I find a tabloid headline screaming, "Angry Trucker Fires Five Shots into UFO!" Now I'm not edgy or antsy, I'm curious, amused, entertained. My nightmare is over, I am *accepting* the moment I'm in, and the story of this bit is complete.

Except for the twist – which, remember, is just a matter of turning an attitude back on itself. Here I am, happily reading about the trucker and the UFO (surprise! there was alcohol involved). I'm blissfully oblivious to the people in line behind me... and boy am I pissing them off!

So that's interesting: Your bit has a twist when the acceptance you arrive at creates rejection for somebody else.

Well, there you have it, a story-driven strategy for building a bit. It's not the only strategy out there, but it's one you can rely on to help you build bits out of nothing at all. Just project yourself into any conceivable situation, figure out how you'd feel if you were there, and then explosively change that feeling into something – anything – else.

Give it a try. Build some bits according to this strategy and see what you get. These, remember, are the component parts:

Setup. Establish the situation and your opposition to it. Take your time here. You're driving your jokes with a potent emotion – rejection – so make the most of it.

Pivot. Introduce a new piece of information that triggers a change in emotional state. Play with the emotional turmoil that's always present when things are in flux.

Transformation. Enter and explore the new emotional state. Take your time here, too; really bask in the wonderfulness of your new attitude.

Twist. Turn the good outcome for you into a bad outcome for somebody else.

So yeah, that's easy.

But let's make it easier still by considering **pain points**.

A pain point is just a thing that makes you suffer in any sense. Pain points, of course, abound in our lives. They can be found in the flickering fluorescent lights of our workplace, where Halitosis Hal, our boss, stands way too close and talks way too loud. They live in tax forms and traffic jams and doctor visits. Once I had a raspberry seed stuck in my tooth for five hours. Pain point? I thought I would go insane! (In fairness, I was tripping balls at the time, so that made it somewhat worse.)

Write down some of your pain points. I know you have plenty to choose from, because, hey, everybody does.

Here are a few of my pain points, just off the top of my (lamentably bald) head: my current cash flow; my sore back; unreliable people; poor craftsmanship; cynical injustice; itchy, dry skin; and this one key on my keyboard that keeps stickingggggggggggggggg.

All of these pain points, plus the rest of mine and all of yours, are potential bits. Each and every one can be driven through an arc of change from rejection to acceptance.

There's a barky dog in our neighbor's apartment and with that incessant yapping we'll never get to sleep. We are so irritated. Then, suddenly – *miraculous pivot* – the dog shuts up. All is silent and, for a moment, we are content. Except that we still can't sleep. So we bang on the wall again, setting off the dog again, because – surprise – it turns out that we need the noise of a barky dog in order to drift off. Now all we have to do is start snoring and wait for the neighbors to be pissed off about that.

For the record, this is only the structure for the jokes, not the jokes themselves. We need the structure, though, because jokes are like shiny ornaments on a Christmas tree and without the structure all we have are a bunch of shiny ornaments all over the floor.

As you play with this structure, you'll notice that you need not go exclusively from a bad feeling to a good one. You can also go the other way around. *Bobby and Sally are two horny teenagers with the house all to themselves. Man, are they feeling great – right up until the moment (pivot) when Sally's father comes home. Now Sally's collapsing in a panic and Bobby's jumping out a window.*

The fact is that you can pivot from any emotion or mindset to any other emotion or mindset – anything you can think of, without limitation.

And now that you know where to look for bits (in pain points) and how to build them (through arcs of change across pivots), why you can develop new bits until you're blue in the face – and then write a bit about that!

RECAP

- ➢ Build a bit on the shift between emotional states
- ➢ Use pivots to trigger emotional change
- ➢ Use pain points to find comedy in everything

That was a good chapter, wasn't it? Wait'll you get a load of the next one. Best one in the whole book. Life changing. You'll see.

11~ PRACTICAL JOKES

Of course no discussion of standup comedy or any comedy would be complete without a thorough discussion of practical jokes.

RECAP

- ➢ Comedy lives in the defeat of expectation
- ➢ Practical jokes are annoying
- ➢ Self-indulgence is its own reward

12~ FIRST FIVE

There's a difference between *defining* yourself and *explaining* yourself.

When you're defining yourself, you're saying, "This is the person I am."

When you're explaining yourself, you're saying, "This is the justification for the person I am."

A lot of standups get lost in this space. They feel like they have to prove they belong – but that just makes them look needy, and the neediness strains their act. If this is an issue for you, just make it your goal to define, not explain. Reveal yourself to everyone, but don't feel like you have to justify yourself to anyone – because you don't.

Be open to the experience you're in and ready to own your point of view. Never wonder if you belong. Your presence proves you belong. And once you acquire this "I belong" frame of mind, you're ready to blow the world away.

When standups speak of a "tight first five," this is what they're talking about: five minutes of material that's not only solid and funny but that really tells the truth of their experience. Here are some things to think about as you undertake this rewarding challenge...

Talk about yourself. Your solid first five is your chance to tell people who you are. Grab that chance! It can be scary to self-reveal, but the situation you're in demands it, because there's only one thing you know that the audience doesn't know, and that's *what it's like to be you.* Fortunately, that's all they really want to know. While you're onstage, they are voyeurs to your experience. If you don't let them know who you really are, you're cheating them of that experience, and they will not be your friend.

Build a robust topic list. Mine yourself for material. All your loves and hates, joys and fears. Regrets from the past. High points of your life. Pain points, as discussed. Jobs you've held. Jobs you've fled. Deep secrets. Heart's desires. Heartfelt beliefs. Claw and scrape your way down deep into your soul – experience the agony and the ecstasy of being you! Or... you can do it the easy way and just write down *25 Interesting Things About Me That Most People Don't Know.* That'll give you more than enough raw material right there.

Hunt for treasure. Your topic list is now your treasure map. Explore everything you find and have fun with it. Use your tools – the tools in this book and the ones you've created or know – to turn the truth of your experience into jokes. What you're looking for – the buried treasure of the topic list – is material that's both **funny *and* authentic.** Keep adding new jokes and measuring them against this standard. Your set is now in workshop form, where quantity is king and practice makes progress. Add, revise, cut, restate, edit, expand, trim, repeat. Never imagine that you have enough material. Always be a glutton for new content that hits the vital sweet spot of funny plus real.

Challenge your work, challenge yourself. Keep asking of every joke in every version of your set, "Is this joke funny and authentic?" If it's not both then it's not there yet, so keep working. Remember, your solid first five is not "a problem to be solved once and for all." It's more dynamic than that. It changes and grows as it reveals to you more and more possibilities and you turn those possibilities into new changes, new growth and new jokes. Lean into this. Be eager to tear everything down and rebuild it again, not because the premises or jokes don't work but because a/ they can always work better and b/ that's where your growth lies. Edit yourself vigorously; let others edit you, too. In diligently building your fabulous first five, you're giving yourself a rich opportunity to lift up your self-understanding right along with your skills.

Find your controlling ideas. As your set starts to take shape and change shape, certain ideas will emerge that make you go, "Yeah, that's me, that's fundamentally who I am." These are the jokes that land closest to your *voice*, and you can now recognize them as the controlling ideas of your work. Identify them, expand upon them, keep feeding them back into your work and keep shaping new jokes around them. This is how you refine your solid first five to the point where everything you say about yourself is essential to who you are. When you reach that level of purity in the work – *wow, this is really about me and honestly about me* – that's when you're getting good to go. And I get that it's hard to make everything both funny *and* honest, but if you settle for less you'll be selling yourself short, so don't.

Make it a discussion. While you're "acquiring" your set (learning it and figuring out how to deliver it), things can come to feel forced, wooden or dull. This mostly happens when material is memorized and recited rather than simply shared. But keep working and you'll work through it. Soon enough you'll get to a place where you're so well-rehearsed that you don't even sound rehearsed. That's the place to be. Your act is not a petrified script but a living, breathing explication of yourself. It thrives not in the space of "I can spit out these jokes I've learned" but rather in the space of "I have total information mastery over all of this." It takes work to gain this mastery, but are you not prepared to do real work in service of your craft? There's something in it for you: five minutes of heart that lands hard.

Brace for impact. You have set yourself the goal of writing your solid first five. When you achieve that goal, you're going to feel kinda high, and that's for several reasons. First, you spoke your truth and got it off your chest – so cathartic. Second, you kept your commitment to yourself, got to see yourself as someone who *can do*. That's a big closed loop in a virtuous circle. Third, you got the endorphin rush of making people laugh. Fourth, most impactfully, in order to make your truths funny, you have had to exaggerate them, energize them and reveal them to yourself. So now you're face-to-face with all of these exaggerated, energized and revealed truths! You're seeing yourself more clearly, more deeply. That's what gets you high. You're injecting authenticity into your practice and craft. You are becoming more *you*.

And *you* is a mighty, mighty thing.

One thing before we move on. If you've ever played video games then you know of things called "Easter eggs," special treats embedded in the game to reward avid players. Here's my Easter egg for you, avid player: Send me your fabulous first five and I will review it, and give you my sense of which jokes are both funny and real, and which are only funny or only real. That's a top edit by a top editor, and it's yours free of charge, just because.

RECAP

- ➢ Build your solid first five around a strong pillar of self
- ➢ Relentlessly refine, revise and replace
- ➢ Take the win and revel in your deep self-knowledge

13~ *POCHEMU NYET?*

I was in Moscow once, adapting an American situation comedy for Russian TV, when one of my Russian writers made a shockingly anti-Semitic joke. "Well, you should know that I'm Jewish," I said. He just gave me a blank stare. "I mean," I continued, "if I were homosexual, would you feel comfortable making gay jokes?"

I will never forget his answer. *"Pochemu nyet?"* Why not?

Well, why not? Doesn't every comic own their own jokes, even if crude or disapproved? Isn't that what comedy is for? To subvert, upset, disrupt, destroy?

Sure, yeah, comedy can do that. It's no secret that comedy has power. Actually, comedy has many powers. It can tickle, amuse, poke, provoke, rile, anger, change minds, change lives, change the world. That's *mojo*. Big power. Big enough to matter. Big enough to demand that each of us ask, "Well, how shall I use this power of mine?"

Broadly speaking, you can use your mojo in one of two ways – to lift up or knock down – and you get to decide which. This isn't exactly like saying, "I choose or choose not to work blue," which can be a strategic choice based on your audience. This is more a question of spirit: Does yours look up or look down?

For many reasons, some cultural and some personal, my Russian colleague's spirit looked down. The joke he made, in the context that he made it, made perfect sense and was perfectly acceptable to him.

Is it acceptable to you? Looking past political correctness, can you detect the basic way that your own work works? In the normal course of your comedy, do you attack or do you embrace, hate or love, lift up or knock down?

Not everyone's a lifter-upper and that's fine; someone's got to slay the sacred cows around here. That I'm an avid lifter-upper will come as no surprise to anyone, but if you're a knocker-downer, more power to you. Your choices are your choices and you get to make them.

Still, it's a mess – well, it can be – figuring out how to navigate social norms. Should you follow them? Ignore them? Transgress them? Stay within them? Step outside them? Shine a mocking light on them? And how can you do any of these things with confidence when "the rules" can change from club to club, from audience to audience, even from week to week? Landmines abound, and the danger of stepping on them is real, for like the sign says, "The trouble with too far is you never know you're going till you've gone."

But now we can skirt this danger, because now we can take our hot-potato topics – punching down, stereotyping, ridiculing, body shaming, bullying, racism, sexism, genderism and everything else – and examine them through a different lens.

We can ask of every joke *will this lift up or knock down?*

If you have a joke that knocks down, and you've previously made the choice to be a lifter-upper, then you will have no trouble knowing that this joke is not right for you. On the other hand, if your comic filter is *attack! attack!* you're not going to play nice, nor should you.

Either way, your choice is now not based on "what they think" but on who you know yourself to be and what you want your comedy to be.

Even so, there will be times when you draw heat for your material, in ways that may surprise you. So whether you're the sort of standup who courts disaster or one who'd rather play it safe, here's how to touch touchy subjects without getting torched.

Turn the joke on yourself. Speaking of Moscow, I was there also when Phil Rosenthal was shooting a documentary about making his TV show *Everybody*

Loves Raymond in Russia. My Russian colleagues thought he was out to make fools of them, but he fooled them and made a fool of himself instead. That trick always works. If you want to mock something, simply view it through the filter of, "Guess I'm not smart enough to understand this." You can attack almost anything if it looks like you're attacking yourself, or just generally bewildered by the topic at hand.

Have a point. If you're skating out on the edge, sensible people will wonder why. For example, are you just being vulgar for the sake of shock value, or do you actually have something to say about how language gets used and abused? If the latter, then I say, "Fuck propriety, do what you want." That's a joke, but also it's true: When you serve the higher purpose of making a point, you deal yourself extra permission to trade in touchy subjects. (See George Carlin's "Seven Words You Can Never Say on Television," if you don't already know it by heart.)

Honor your topic. If there's a dangerous subject you want to confront, you can always ease yourself into it just by showing respect. Honor your topic. Explore it, investigate it, experience it. Go at it with curiosity, even wide-eyed wonder. Your good intent goes a long way toward winning friends in controversial spaces, and you can telegraph this intent by making it clear that you're not there to harm or mock, just to learn. Weirdly, the less you seem to be judging a topic, the more judgmental you can be. I would offer God as an example. A lot of people don't think God is okay, but I do, and now that I've approved of God, I can tell you all the things They consistently get wrong. (I've just changed God's pronouns, by the way, and about damn time I'd say.)

Come clean fast. Sometimes you step on a landmine. You know? You just do. You tell the wrong joke to the wrong audience at the wrong time – *boom!* – your foot is a bloody stump. Don't fight it, and especially don't deny it. Accept it, own it and move on. The sooner you acknowledge your swing-and-a-miss, the sooner everyone can get back to having a good time. If you don't do this, you create an uncomfortable air of apprehension and make it hard for the audience to stay supportive of you and willing to engage with your act.

Acknowledge mistakes. In almost any context, mistakes are better acknowledged than denied. Actually, when you deny a mistake, you're behaving like characters in sitcoms, who repeatedly hurt themselves with mistakes and then hurt themselves again by denying the mistakes they just made. That's how sitcom works, and that's fine, but here in the real world you're far better off admitting your mistakes. That way they can only hurt you once. Especially with an audience – they can be so fickle – it's just good practice to own up right away.

Embrace change. Norms do change, and sometimes for the better. If you originally wrote a joke or a bit that was in harmony with a social attitude that has since shifted, it's kind of up to you to rethink or replace the joke based on what you find around you now. This is not to say that you have to surrender your viewpoint or pander to the crowd's, but if your goal is to win over your audience, it won't help you to demand that the audience hold different views than they do. Accept reality – embrace change – and your act will continue to be fresh, new and relevant to your world.

This is especially challenging for oldsters like me. My worldview was shaped in the 1960s and 1970s, a time that seems archaic today, almost quaint. Words that were commonplace back in the day – retard, tomboy, sissy – are shunned now. Rightly so, say I; however, rightly or wrongly, I am an old man living in a new reality, and if I want to prosper within it, then I simply have to adapt.

You want your act to have power. I want my act to have power. We know that if we have power we will have influence, and we really want to have influence. But with influence comes, you know, a certain amount of responsibility. For pure clarity in this realm, just strive to create jokes you can believe in and then stand behind the jokes you create. That way you can be sure of, at least, using your power in harmony with your worldview and your intent.

RECAP

- Comedy has power
- Use your power strategically
- Own your point of view but be respectful of others'

14~ SET YOURSELF A CHALLENGE

Just now I'm setting myself the challenge to come up with additional strategies that I can share with you to make your standup practice more effective and fun. I don't have to do this. No one will miss this content if it's not there – how could they? But I like to set challenges and I like to meet them, and I especially like to model this approach, so here are some extra bonus tips for the healthy practice of standup.

Set yourself a challenge. Any challenge, any time. I just did it and I feel good. If you do it, you will feel good, too. Plus you will be practicing your craft and that's never not good. This strategy is especially handy for times when you feel like nothing else productive can get done – like when you're sitting around waiting for the phone to ring or the email to ding. Don't just sit there! Set a challenge, meet the challenge and come away feeling stronger and better about yourself.

Write from a different perspective. When we write jokes, we naturally think about how they'll sound when we tell them, and we say them out loud to hear how they'll sound. That's fine, but this does mean that we're always writing jokes through and for our own voice, and that can get stale. Refresh your writing by writing jokes from the perspective of someone other than you – your mother, your dog, your evil twin – just to mix things up. When you write from a different perspective, you change the sorting system in your brain and open a whole new trove of jokes that you'd never discover any other way.

Load up on knowledge. Another way to reboot your humor is just to load in new facts – buckets of them, about anything at all. I don't know if you kids remember libraries, but I used to go into them, grab books at random and absorb whatever passed beneath my eyeballs. Then I turned that stuff into stories or jokes or whatever. It's simple, really: New information means new ideas and new ideas mean new jokes.

Don't stop at the first joke. When we're looking for jokes to serve certain purposes, we often stop as soon as we find one that does the job. But why stop? Why not solve the same problem more times than once? Maybe many more times. This pushes your practice, which is good, but it also strengthens your faith. You'll trust your jokes more when you know that they beat out so many worthy contenders to fill a vital role in your act.

Add skills. Whatever it is that you consider yourself to be – a standup comic, an actor or a writer, a hobbyist or professional – constantly be asking yourself, "What can I add to my bag of tricks? What else can I learn how to do?" Maybe try voice-over or ventriloquism, sketch or improv, even macramé, the ancient mariner's art of knot tying. Do it just for the learning that's in it. Always be seeking to venture into new realms of interest and expertise. Become more than you are, for versatility is a great – and profitable – quality to have.

Draw a cartoon. I know you think you'll suck at this. I suck, too. But why shouldn't we draw cartoons? Is it a part of "funny" that we're not allowed into? That's bullshit. So draw. Draw crudely if you have to, but draw to explore the difference between jokes that work on the stage and ones that work on the page, or ones that work when heard versus ones that have to be seen. If nothing else, this will expand your practice in a new direction, and as we already know, just because you do standup doesn't mean you can't do other things, too.

Make lists. By now it's no secret that I love lists. More than that, I admire them. Lists are the ultimate creative hack: They take so little effort and yield so much useful content. They also don't vex the ego 'cause, you know, they're just lists, so you never have to worry if the words are pretty or even spelled right. With lists you can really let yourself go. So if you're creatively lazy or in any way blocked, lean on lists for everything. They never fail to bear fruit.

Teach what you know. It's also no secret by now that I think teaching is magic. Every time I teach I learn, even unto the umpteenth time I've taught. If you fancy that you *can't* teach, well, you're just wrong. Even sitting down with a friend and explaining how your jokes work, that's going to be interesting information for them and just a pot of gold for you. Try it, you'll see. Then do much more. Teach groups, classes, whatever. Sometimes it's good for your wallet, but always it's good for your soul. So have at it. Why not? Everyone's a teacher in some sense; you might as well be one in yours.

Exploit reality. Of course there's funny to be found all around you, in the people you know and the places you're at. No doubt you already use these resources, but if you use them more methodically – really acquire the habit of mining adjacent reality for jokes – two good things will happen. First, you'll have more material; always good. Second, by searching for the funny everywhere, you'll improve your power to find it anywhere.

Stay in your practice. It's much harder to start a practice than to keep one going, so once you've got yours established, you really want to keep it chugging along. To accomplish this, just don't put all your eggs in one basket. Have lots of projects going on: many different bits and sets in various stages of development; diverse booking opportunities on the horizon; new parts of your craft to explore; new skills to take on. If you have lots going on, then when one part of your practice slows down or dies out, you'll still have other parts – active and thriving parts – that can help keep your practice in gear.

Break it down. Whenever you have a problem you can't solve, break it down into smaller problems that you can solve. For example, if you're trying to write a bit that is funny and has a story, but neither is quite working right, you can run into trouble trying to fix the funny and the story at the same time. Break it down. First work out the story, then lay in the funny. Everything works better when you work it in steps.

Procrastinate later. If there's work to be done, do it now. Once you're in possession of both the tools and the time to do standup, you're ready to be in your practice... so *be in your practice*. Don't waste time wondering whether you deserve to be in your practice, or whether people respect and accept you for being there. You're there. Be working. Remember that any urge to stall or delay a task is really just about fear, so fight the urge – or at least save it for after the work is done.

Be good to people. Standup comedy can be a tragic occupation, shot through with sadness, anger, misanthropy, conflict, narcissism, paranoia and rage.

Many of these emotions are the fuel that drives the artform, but they don't always make for a warm and fuzzy workplace. When you're in your workplace, don't yield to bad vibes – instead, give off good ones. This will be to your direct benefit, because the more positivity you create, the more positivity there is all around you, and thus more positivity for you bask in and enjoy.

Be about something. Even if you think you're only about "making them laugh," you can always be about that and about something else as well. Your jokes aren't just your gags, they're also your thoughts – your ideas, insights, perspectives, beliefs – and you have ownership of them. If you have a truth to express, express it. If you have an urgent itch to scratch, scratch it. Imagine that you have the power to change the world with your voice because, in fact, you do.

Save everything. If all goes according to plan, you're in for a long and mighty career, and over the course of that career you just won't believe how much of your material you'll end up reusing, retooling, recycling and restoring. (Keen students of my work will see the many jokes that I've recycled here.) So start your stockpile now. Save what you create, even if you think it's crap, because it's all part of your body of work, and your body of work is a resource that you'll draw upon your whole life long.

Take the long view. My creative practice dates back half a century now. I had no idea when I started out just how much time and opportunity lay ahead of me. If you're just starting out, or even a bit further along, I hope you will take it from me that the road ahead will be fruitful and littered with gifts. Just take the long view, practice patience, and draw yourself into your future, one effective and productive day at a time.

RECAP

> - Keep setting and meeting new challenges
> - Plan to make a difference
> - Advance your growth and keep your practice in gear

15~ HAPPY WHERE YOU ARE

If you have come this far in this book, I imagine that a few changes have taken place. You're probably more objective, constructive and productive. You may have a deeper and clearer sense of yourself. I trust that you've advanced in your craft and I hope that you're hitting new high water marks in your career, even if modest ones. You're in your practice and on your path, and I am happy to have helped you be where you are.

With that said, be on the lookout for what they call "a revolution of rising expectations." When people experience positive and rewarding growth, they tend to want more of it right away. If they don't get it – if they encounter temporary setbacks or plateaus – it can feel more frustrating than if they'd never had that growth in the first place. If you experience one of these funks, just hang in there. Remember that all growth is good growth and yours will resume in the fullness of time.

Don't believe me? Dude, I'm in my seventh decade! I'm experiencing growth every minute of every day, and it takes me by surprise *all the fricking time!* I would have thought that by the time I "got old" I would have settled down and stopped this relentless pursuit of my craft. That hasn't happened. It's never happened. And can I tell you the truth? I feel like as long as I'm in relentless pursuit of my craft, I can easily call my life a success.

Same with you, same with you. You might not get the trappings you want (all that fame, money, glory), but you'll have your practice, and this can sustain you and make you happy down through the long years. Take it from someone at this end of those long years.

Speaking of long years, I also want to reinforce that you just won't believe how much you will do in the course of your creative career. How much content you'll churn out. How many great moments you'll have. How many highs and triumphs. How many small and big wins. How many jokes, jokes, jokes, jokes, jokes. And all you have to do to get them is to do the *one damn thing* that you want to do anyway, which is to just keep after it.

Are you a professional comedian? Do you call yourself a recreational one? That's fine; standup comedy is grandly recreational, and even if you never make a dime doing it, you can still enjoy it as a thrilling avocation. As the COVID pandemic revealed when comics thronged to Zoom mics in droves, the world will not deny you a stage.

Nor should it. For your purposes, any stage will do. Maybe you want bigger ones, better paying ones, more appreciation, more validation, all of that. Those are great goals to shoot for, but never forget that what you're doing is supposed to be fun. In times when you find that it's *not* fun, it's probably because you're not satisfied with where you are.

Maybe you think I'm going to say, "For your peace of mind, be satisfied with where you are."

Or maybe you think I'm going to say, "If you can't be satisfied with where you are, go find better mics."

Actually, I'm going to say both.

Be satisfied with where you are. Make the most of every mic and appreciate each one for what it is: a chance to share you mirth and worth with the world. Cherish being in the present you're in. That's just basic, the bedrock strategy for having a happy life: be happy where you are.

But also push yourself harder, because the harder you push yourself, the richer your rewards will be and the yet more profound happiness you can enjoy. Accept and challenge, challenge and accept. That's what makes a life rise.

One thing that gets in the way of all this is the expectation that we place on ourselves when we look at ourselves through others' eyes. Holding yourself up to their expectations is a sure path to frustration, just as comparing your progress to their progress is a fool's paradigm. You're on the path you're on. *Be* on the path you're on.

I'll do the same. I never know from book to book where my next book will come from or where it will take me, but I'm in my practice and I'm on my path, so I figure I can't go too far wrong. These days, at my age, my life's motto is *finish hard!* I seem to be doing that now.

This book, like most of my books, comes with my famous, patented **Five-Minute Promise**. As you advance in your practice, you might run into challenges I can help you meet or questions I can help you address. When that happens, just reach out to me at john.vorhaus@gmail.com. I promise to help you in any way I can, to the full extent of my ability – so long as it doesn't take more than five minutes and I don't have to leave my desk. As my many years of keeping this promise have demonstrated, there's a fair amount of good I can do in five minutes sitting at my desk. So reach out. For as long as I'm here, I'm here for you.

More later, -jv

~ ABOUT THE AUTHOR

John Vorhaus reckons that he's written a thousand "about the author" blurbs in his life, and he can't hardly face writing one more. So he'll cut to the chase: lives in California; happily married forever; must have dogs; does art, writing, poker, consulting, anything else he thinks of. Business model is and always has been, *walk down the beach, pick up everything you find and turn it into a party hat.*